Contents

WALK THIS WAY

Ephesians

by Bryson Smith

MATTHIAS MEDIA

Walk This Way
© Matthias Media 1996, 2001

Published in the UK by
THE GOOD BOOK COMPANY
Elm House, 37 Elm Road
New Malden, Surrey KT3 3HB
Tel: 020-8942-0880
Fax: 020-8942-0990
e-mail: admin@thegoodbook.co.uk
Website: www.thegoodbook.co.uk

ISBN 1-873166-21-4

Cover Illustrations: Richard Knight

How to make the most of these studies

1. What is an Interactive Bible Study?

These 'interactive' Bible studies are a bit like a guided tour of a famous city. The studies will take you through Paul's letter to the Ephesians, pointing out things along the way, filling in background details, and suggesting avenues for further exploration. But there is also time for you to do some sight-seeing of your own—to wander off, have a good look for yourself, and form your own conclusions.

In other words, we have designed these studies to fall half-way between a sermon and a set of unadorned Bible study questions. We want to provide stimulation and input and point you in the right direction, while leaving you to do a lot of the exploration and discovery yourself.

We hope that these studies will stimulate lots of 'interaction'— interaction with the Bible, with the things we've written, with your own current thoughts and attitudes, with other people as you discuss them, and with God as you talk to him about it all.

2. The format

Each study contains sections of text to introduce, summarize, suggest and provoke. We've left plenty of room in the margins for you to jot comments and questions as you read. Interspersed throughout the text are three types of 'interaction', each with their own symbol:

For starters

Questions to break the ice and get you thinking.

Investigate

Questions to help you investigate key parts of the Bible.

Think it Through

Questions to help you think through the implications of your discoveries and write down your own thoughts and reactions.

When you come to one of these symbols, you'll know that it's time to do some work of your own.

3. Suggestions for Individual Study

- Before you begin, pray that God would open your eyes to what he is saying in this letter and give you the spiritual strength to do something about it. You may be spurred to pray again at the end of the study.
- Before you start, it's a good idea to read right through Ephesians in one sitting, to get a feel for the direction and content of the letter as a whole.
- Work through the study, following the directions as you go. Write in the spaces provided.
- Resist the temptation to skip over the *Think it through* sections. It is important to think about the sections of text (rather than just accepting them as true) and to ponder the implications for your life. Writing these things down is a very valuable way to get your thoughts working.
- Take what opportunities you can to talk to others about what you've learnt.

4. Suggestions for Group Study

- Much of the above applies to group study as well. The studies are suitable for structured Bible study or cell groups, as well as for more informal pairs and threesomes. Get together with a friend/s and work through them at your own pace; use them as the basis for regular Bible study with your spouse. You don't need the formal structure of a 'group' to gain maximum benefit.

- It is *vital* that group members work through the study themselves *before* the group meets. The group discussion can take place comfortably in an hour (depending on how side-tracked you get!), but only if all the members have done the work and are familiar with the material.

- Spend most of the group time discussing the 'interactive' sections—*Investigate* and *Think it through*. Reading all the text together will take too long and should be unnecessary if the group members have done their preparation. You may wish to underline and read aloud particular paragraphs or sections of text that you think are important.

- The role of the group leader is to direct the course of the discussion and to try to draw the threads together at the end. This will mean a little extra preparation—underlining important sections of text to emphasize, working out which questions are worth concentrating on, and being sure of the main thrust of the study. Leaders will also probably want to work out approximately how long they'd like to spend on each part.

- We haven't included an 'answer guide' to the questions in the studies. This is a deliberate move. We want to give you a guided tour of these intiguing sayings of the Lord Jesus, not a lecture. There is more than enough in the text we have written and the questions we have asked to point you in what we think is the right direction. The rest is up to you.

Need more help? Get the tapes...

If you would like some additional input, there is a series of tapes available that expound the relevant passages. The series of 8 talks costs £10 in a boxed set (plus 80p for postage and packing). Another set of tapes deals specifically with the complex ideas raised in chapter 1. *We've got it all!* is also a series of 8 talks costing £10 in a boxed set (plus 80p for postage and packing).

To order, call us at The Good Book Company on 020-8942-0880.

1

You've got it all

David looked disappointedly round the room. Numbers were down for Bible study tonight. Some of the group were away on holidays. Some had to work back at the office. Some were sick. All valid reasons, but David couldn't help feeling disappointed. Three Christians sitting together in a lounge seemed so insignificant. But it was too late to cancel the night now, so with just a hint of weariness in his voice David opened proceedings: "Let's open in prayer."

Sometimes being a Christian can seem pretty ordinary. That's why the apostle Paul's letter to the church at Ephesus is such a great part of the Bible. When we read Ephesians our eyes are opened to the awe-inspiring dimensions of what God has done for us in Christ. It's as if the apostle Paul leads us to the edge of a lookout and stretches out in front of us the enormous view of God's plans for the universe, and where we as Christians fit into that plan. The size and the scope of the view just becomes more and more mind-boggling the further we read.

A letter like Ephesians, therefore, tells our friend David that no matter how small his Bible study group is, being a Christian is never insignificant. Being a Christian is radical. Being a Christian puts us with Jesus Christ at the very heart of the universe.

So hold onto your hats as throughout these eight studies we throw ourselves into some of the most profound parts of the New Testament.

Investigate

Read Ephesians 1:1-14

1. Reread verses 3-14. List all the things that God has done for us.

Blessed, chosen, Predestined, adopted, given us
grace in Jesus, Redeemed, Forgiven, wisdom, understanding
The Holy Spirit as a seal

2. Write down what you think is meant by the following words and phrases.

• spiritual blessings (v.3)

Relationship with God - Spiritual connection
Forgiveness

• heavenly realms (v.3)

• predestined (vv.4-5,11)

Previously Chosen - Chosen before our worth could be
Calculated

• adopted (v.4)

Legally his - Permanently his

• redemption (vv.7,14)

bought back

• the mystery of his will (v.9)

His plan for creation Regarding
Forgiveness, Justification

• conformity with the purpose of his will (v.11)

Making him Lord

• for the praise of his glory (vv.12,14)

3. Is there any one spiritual blessing which impresses you more than the rest?

Giving us the Holy Spirit

4. Why do you think Paul mentions so many blessings in this section rather than concentrating on just a couple? What effect does it have on you when you consider all these blessings together?

Wow! makes you feel special, close

What God has done

In some respects, verse 3 is the summary verse for this intense section of Ephesians. God has blessed us with every spiritual blessing. No blessing is lacking; no blessing is overlooked; no blessing is held back. Name a spiritual blessing, any spiritual blessing, and if you're a Christian you've got it.

Notice, however, that the phrase is spiritual blessing, not spiritual gift. There is a difference. Paul is not saying that every Christian is equally gifted for every task. In fact, in Ephesians 3 Paul will say quite the opposite. Christians have a great diversity of gifts. But here in verse 3 Paul is talking about something much more important than gifts. Paul is talking about our spiritual status and intimacy before God, and in that respect every Christian has it all. We cannot be any more treasured and important to God than we already are. We are his forgiven children. We call the Creator of this universe our Father. His Spirit lives in us. We have been lavished with the great secrets of life. These are staggering things that God has done for us.

Putting it all together, these verses tell us that no matter how old you are or what nationality you are or what job you have or what your marital status is, if you're a Christian you've got it all. You do not need anything else spiritually. You are blessed with every spiritual blessing.

Investigate

Reread verses 3-14

1. What role has Jesus had in our receiving spiritual blessings?

He paid our debt and ~~made~~ gave us his ~~that~~ righteousness so we could have fellowship with God

2. What do you think it means to be "in Christ"?

Part of the Body

Statement of Loyalty.

In Christ / ressurected in christ.

3. What role does predestination have? Try and write verses 11-12 in your own words.

He wanted us - so he chose us.

How has God blessed us

We've discovered that we have every spiritual blessing. But how? How has God gone about achieving these privileges for us? The big phrase is: *in Christ* (v.3). In fact in these first 14 verses Jesus' name is mentioned 15 times!

Paul emphasizes that it is only through a relationship with Jesus that we receive these great privileges. The principle is simple; if you don't have Jesus, you don't have the blessings. That's because all these spiritual blessings that Paul mentions come to us through Jesus' work on the cross.

In verse 7, Paul says we were redeemed by Jesus' blood. That happened at the cross when Jesus gave his life as the payment necessary to buy us back from sin. In the same verse we are told of our forgiveness. That happened at the cross when God's anger was poured out onto Jesus so that his mercy could be poured out on us. In verse 5, we are told of our adoption as God's children. The word "adopted" implies we weren't always his children. Something happened that enabled us to be welcomed into God's family. That happened at the cross when Jesus opened the door for a relationship so intimate with God that we can call on him as our Father.

It all happened on the cross. The only reason we have every spiritual blessing is because Jesus gave us every spiritual blessing on the cross.

Unbelievably, that's not all. A new dimension has still to be added. Being "in Christ" incorporates us into God's future plans for creation.

Paul tells us that history is not simply a random collection of happenings. History is the working out of events in conformity to God's will. Creation is heading towards a climax at which everything and everyone will come under the headship of Jesus Christ (vv.9-10). That makes being a Christian very exciting because it puts you at the very centre of God's plans for the future. When you are in Christ, you are already at the place to which all of creation is heading.

Are you starting to see how breathtaking the view is from this chapter? God has done absolutely everything for us. We hold every spiritual blessing. And how has he done this for us? Through Jesus Christ. Jesus' death on the cross showers us with blessings and puts us at the very centre of God's plans for the universe.

One question still remains. Why on earth would God be bothered to do this for us?

Investigate

1. What are some possible reasons why God would bless us so much?

~~He Made us~~

He

2. What reasons does Paul give for God blessing us so much? (vv.4,7,9)

He loves us
His grace is rich
He Wanted to

3. If we were actually chosen before the creation of the world (v.4), to what extent can it depend on our own abilities?

Not at all

Pulling the threads together

In the course of this chapter we have skimmed some of the most magnificent verses in the Bible. Hopefully by this stage you're thinking something like "There's so much packed into this first chapter, I don't think we've really done justice to it." *A brief study like this can't.*

Paul has taken us to the edge of a mountain and he has allowed us to gaze into the vastness of God's plans for the universe. It is a view with Jesus at the centre of everything and with us possessing everything in him. This is a view so breathtaking that it ought to revolutionize our lives.

Being a Christian may be many things but it's never small scale!

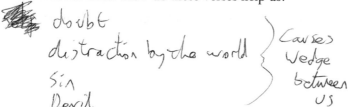

Think it through

1. If we are blessed with every spiritual blessing why is it that we so often feel discontent in our lives? How do these verses help us?

> doubt
> distraction by the world } Causes
> Sin   } Wedge
> Devil   } between
>   us

2. Considering what God has done for us, how do you think we should respond?

> We should emulate him in our relationship to others + be full of thanks to him

3. Do you believe that God really does work out everything in conformity with the purpose of his will? When is it hard to believe this?

> Overall yes.
> This passage concentrates on the will of God. Gods side of the ~~covenant~~ New Covenant. We also have a part to play.

4. "Being a Christian is bad for your self-esteem." Do you agree? What does this passage tell us about ourselves?

> We are very loved.

5. If Christ is at the centre of God's plans for everything, is he at the centre of yours? Given what we have read in Ephesians 1:3-14, what should our priorities in life actually be?

2

Ephesians 1:15-23

Paul at Prayer

It's always fascinating to watch a master craftsman at work–to see a sculptor create a thing of beauty out of a shapeless block; to witness a potter shape an intricate bowl from a lump of clay; to watch an artist putting oil on canvas. It's exciting to kneel next to the apostle Paul as he prays.

Paul is a master of prayer. Paul's prayers have been preserved in the Scriptures more than any other New Testament writer. Listening in on Paul's prayers can help us to pray better, because they reflect a passion, a clarity of thought and a Christ-centredness that is often lacking in our own prayers.

In Ephesians we have now reached one of Paul's prayers, and it may not have just been for the Ephesians. Some of the earliest manuscripts of this letter actually don't have the words "in Ephesus" in verse 1–the letter is simply addressed "to the saints". Furthermore this letter is quite uncharacteristic of Paul because it contains few personal details (compare Rom 16). That's unusual, since Paul had spent a couple of years in Ephesus and would have personally known quite a lot of people in the church. Putting all this together, it is quite possible that this was really a circular letter from Paul designed to be passed around lots of churches. The copy we have translated in our Bibles is simply the copy that was sent to the Ephesian church.

If that is the case what we have in 1:15-23 is the sort of prayer that Paul would pray for all Christians! If Paul were here today these would probably be the sorts of things he would pray for us.

Investigate

Read Ephesians 1:15-16

1. Why does Paul pray?

2. What impression do you get from these verses about Paul's commitment to prayer?

3. What is the first thing that Paul does in his prayer?

Paul's motive for prayer

With his opening phrase, "for this reason...", Paul clearly links his prayer to what he has already written about in verses 3-14. The wonderful truths that we discovered in our last study prompt Paul to pray. Paul is so excited about the Ephesians being blessed with every spiritual blessing (1:3) that he wants to thank God for his generosity.

Paul's example is instructive. Often our prayers resemble cosmic shopping lists as we ask God to help us through numerous problems. Health, employment, good marks at college or school, family issues, having enough money in the bank: these are the sorts of things we usually fill our prayers with. That's all right to a degree. All these things have their place and it's not as if God doesn't want us to pray about these things. But if our prayers are always preoccupied with these issues it may be that we need to learn a lesson from Paul. Maybe we don't fully understand how much God has already done for us in Christ. God has already been so generous in blessing us with every spiritual blessing that our prayers should be overflowing with thanksgiving.

Investigate

Read Ephesians 1:17-23

1. What does Paul ask God for in verses 17-18? What three reasons does Paul give for asking for this? (vv.18b-19)

2. Why do you think Paul wants the Ephesians to know and experience God's power? (compare 3:16-17)

3. In verse 19-23, Paul describes an example of God's power at work. Look up Romans 1:4 and 1 Corinthians 6:14 for more of the same. In the context of Paul's prayer, how do these examples give us encouragement?

Paul's prayer list

This is an intense prayer. Paul is basically asking God to help the Ephesians to grow in their understanding of what God has done for them in Christ. He wants God to convict the Ephesians of the things he has told them about in the first fourteen verses. Indeed in the light of those verses, what else would you pray? God's purpose for all of creation is that it be under the headship of Christ and by his sheer mercy alone God has shaped history so as to save us in Christ. These are truths which reflect God's agenda for this world. It is no surprise that Paul prays for the Ephesians to grasp these things, to view reality from God's perspective.

Paul's prayer is a good one for us to imitate. We ought to fill our prayers with requests for God to enlighten us so that we might come to understand and appreciate all that he has done for us in Christ. And when God answers that sort of prayer and we start to comprehend the dimensions of what we have in Christ, life can never be the same again. When we understand the incomparably great power of what God has done for us, we are lifted out of our small-mindedness and our spiritual apathy. It puts our earthly cares and desires into proportion.

God has blessed us in the heavenly realms with every spiritual blessing in Christ. That should revolutionize our lives. At the very least it should fill our prayers.

Think it through

1. Have a look at some of Paul's other prayers (e.g. Phil 1:9-11; Col 1:9-14; 2 Thess 1:11-12). What new things do you discover about the way Paul prays?

2. Think back over your prayers for the past few days/weeks. What has been your motive to pray? What have you prayed about? How do your prayers compare with that of Paul's in Ephesians 1?

3. What do you feel is the main thing we can learn from Paul about prayer?

4. "But it's different for Paul. He's an apostle, a super Christian. I'm just an average person. There's no way I could pray the way Paul does."
Do you agree? Why/why not?

5. Are there things in your life at the moment which a clearer understanding "of the riches of his glorious inheritance" would help?

6. Use Paul's prayer in Ephesians as a model and pray the same sorts of things for Christians you know. Writing it down in full, or as bullet points might help...

3

Ephesians 2:1-22

From Rags to Riches

People love rags to riches stories. Our hearts warm when we hear about someone who starts out with nothing, but through hard work and determination beats the odds, grabs an opportunity and makes a success of things. The person who builds up a business from scratch, or who starts as a waiter and ends up owning a chain of restaurants—we love those sorts of stories because they capture our imagination and our aspirations.

In study 1, we discovered that Ephesians opens with a cosmic bang as Paul paints a massive picture of God's plans for the universe. We discovered how we as Christians have been blessed with every spiritual blessing. In Ephesians 2 Paul continues to explain the grandeur of our salvation by describing what we used to be before we had every spiritual blessing. It is a rags to riches story like no other.

Investigate

Read Ephesians 2:1-10. These verses can be divided into 3 main sections.

1. "You were..."

a. How does Paul describe the Ephesians before they became Christians?

b. What are some of the "ways of the world?" (v.2-3)

2. "...but now you are..."

a. How does Paul describe the Ephesians after they have become Christians?

b. In verse 6, Paul writes in the past tense. The Ephesians are already seated with Jesus in the heavenly realms. Does this make sense? How?

3. "...because..."

a. How has this transformation from spiritual rags to riches taken place?

b. What should be the Ephesians' response?

Making peace with God

'But' can be such a great word! 'There's been a car accident but no one has been hurt.' 'I lost my wallet but it was returned with all the money still in it.' 'My alarm didn't go off but I still caught the bus.' The word 'but' often introduces some good news when things are looking bleak. Thank God that Ephesians 2:4 starts with a 'but'!

In verses 1-3, Paul describes the desperate situation of not knowing Christ. It is a picture of death, slavery and condemnation. Paul then goes on to systematically show how each of these things is reversed in Christ.

Whereas we were dead in sin and transgression, now we have become alive (v.4). Whereas we were enslaved and held captive by evil forces, now we sit on thrones alongside Jesus (v.6). Whereas we were condemned, now we have been saved from condemnation (vv.4-5).

It is an exciting and dramatic picture of what happens when we respond to the gospel. Our spiritual rags of death, slavery and condemnation are replaced with spiritual riches of life, enthronement and salvation.

Paul keeps the most unbelievable thing for last. This rags to riches story is like no other you'll hear. Most rags to riches stories revolve around someone succeeding because of his or her own hard work and determination. But (there's that word again) the amazing message of the gospel is that we are taken from spiritual rags to riches for free. We contribute nothing. It is not our efforts that achieve it; it is God's efforts through Jesus. It is a free gift out of God's sheer mercy and love and grace (vv.8-10).

There's even more to be said. In verses 11-22, Paul gives another perspective on our spiritual rags to riches story. This time he is not so much concerned with our reconciliation with God as with our reconciliation with each other.

Investigate

Read Ephesians 2:11-22. We can examine these under the same headings as the previous verses...

1. "You were..."

    a. How does Paul describe the Ephesians before they knew Christ?

    b. What are "the covenants of the promise"? What used to be the Ephesians relationship to these?

2. "...but now you are..."

    a. How does Paul describe what the Ephesians are now?

    b. Can you discover any more 'buts' in the passage? What do they tell us?

3. "...because..."

    a. How has this transformation happened in the life of the Ephesians? What do you think verses 14-15 mean?

    b. What should be the response of the Ephesians?

Reconciliation with each other

Paul lived in a world where there were only two categories of humanity: Jew and Gentile. Between the two existed great hostility stemming from the Jews' identity as God's people. God had indeed promised Abraham that his descendants would be God's people; but over time the people of Israel became very arrogant and forgot that originally they had been chosen to be a light to all the nations. God wanted the Jews to be a blessing to the Gentiles, but instead the privilege of being God's people became twisted into a self-righteous national pride. The Gentiles were looked down upon with contempt by the Jews; and the Gentiles in turn despised the Jews as obnoxious and self important people. There was no love lost between them.

Against that background of hostility, Paul describes how Jesus Christ has demolished the barrier between Jew and Gentile. In verse 15 he describes how Jesus tore down the wall between Jew and Gentile by abolishing the law with its commandments and regulations. In other words, Jesus' death meant that now anyone could become one of God's people without becoming a Jew. The commandments and regulations were no longer relevant. Because of the cross, both Jew and Gentile could now call on the name of Jesus and be saved. They were now on equal footing. The wall of hostility was down.

Paul doesn't just speak of Jesus tearing something down. Jesus builds something new to replace the old wall of hostility. Jesus has built an entirely new humanity, a new society based on equality before God (vv.15-18).

This perspective opens up a whole new way of looking at things. The struggling little Bible study group we go to, the small prayer meeting we attend, the local church we go along to—they can all seem so small scale and unexciting and full of the strangest people. Yet they are—we are—part of God's new humanity. God's family.

Think it through

1. What are some of the solutions that people suggest to fix the world's problems? What solution do you think Paul would suggest?

2. What walls of hostility do we sometimes build between each other? How does the cross abolish these?

3. What implications does 2:21-22 have for the way we treat each other?

4. Paul has described how we have been given spiritual riches for free at Christ's expense. Where does doing good works fit into the Christian life?

4

Profile of an Apostle

The former United States Secretary of State, James Baker, once said that his job was one of the most glamorous and important jobs in the world. He travelled the globe meeting the most important people and resolving issues which affected all humanity. But one day while being driven in a limousine through Washington D. C., he noticed an old lonely man walking the street. As the car passed by, he recognised the old man as his predecessor. This powerful man realised then that if he continued to look to his job for his identity and fulfilment, then one day he'd be like that lone figure walking the street. Instead Baker went on to anchor his identity in Jesus.

If someone were to ask you to describe who you are, and what 'makes you tick', what would you say?

To whom or to what do you anchor your identity? What makes you feel important? What are the things that you would use to define your life?

In Ephesians 3 we get an intriguing insight into how the apostle Paul thought about himself.

The chapter opens with a phrase that Paul has already used in the letter, "For this reason...". Paul used it back in 1:15, where, after giving this big cosmic picture of how we have received every spiritual blessing in Christ, he exploded with gratitude as he explained how he prayed for the Ephesians in the light of those great spiritual truths. A similar thing is happening in Ephesians 3:1. After writing about how we have been reconciled to both God and each other through Christ (see study 3) Paul just can't contain himself any more. His emotions pour out onto the page as he again explains how these truths lead him to pray for the Ephesians.

Investigate

Read Ephesians 3:1-13

1. List as many things as you can concerning the "mystery" which Paul writes about in these verses.

2. What are the ways in which Paul describes himself in these verses?

3. Paul mentions "grace" at several points. What is he referring to?

4. Who are the rulers and authorities in the heavenly realms in verse 10? (see also 6:12)

5. Considering your answer to 4, try and write verse 10 in your own words.

6. In what sense are Paul's sufferings the glory of the Ephesians (v.13)?

How Paul portrays himself

In some respects verses 2-13 are almost an aside to Paul's main train of thought. It's as if mentioning being a prisoner (v.1) and maybe also the Gentiles (v.1) jogs Paul's mind to go off and talk about his role as an apostle to the Gentiles. In verse 14, however, Paul returns to his original thought as he continues, "For this reason...".

Whether these verses are an aside or not, they give us a powerful insight into Paul. In particular these verses display how Paul is totally captivated by the greatness of Jesus Christ and the immense importance of the gospel. Paul doesn't describe himself in terms of his own talent or family background. He doesn't get his identity and significance from income or academic record. Paul thinks about himself in terms of Jesus Christ. Jesus and the gospel dominate his thinking and lifestyle and self-expression.

Investigate

Read Ephesians 3:14-21

1. What does Paul pray for the Ephesians?

2. What are the similarities between this prayer and the prayer in 1:15-23?

3. Paul specifically mentions the three persons of the Trinity. What distinctive things does he say of each?

4. What does it mean to be "rooted and established in love" (v.17)?

How Paul prays for others

After discovering that Paul thinks about himself in terms of Jesus Christ, it is no surprise that when praying for the Ephesians he asks that they would know Jesus better (vv.17-18). This shows how much Paul is captivated by the gospel. The rags to riches story of chapter 2 is not simply a pleasing idea for Paul, like dreaming of what you would do if you won the lottery. It is a profound life-changing event. When Paul talks about himself, he talks about Jesus. When Paul prays, he asks that others would better understand Jesus, and that Jesus would live in their hearts and shape their life.

Does the gospel dominate us the way it does Paul? It should.

In one sense Paul had a unique place in God's purposes. He was commissioned by God to be the apostle to the Gentiles. We don't have that in common with him. But what we do have in common with Paul is this: we were dead in our sins but in Christ we have been made alive. When you see life in those terms, there is nothing more important than knowing Jesus and making him known.

Think it through

1. What things do we use to give meaning and significance to our lives?

2. What things in life distract us from the true importance of Jesus Christ and the gospel?

3. What sort of features would characterize a person who is "rooted and established in love"? Try and be as specific as possible.

4. Think of some practical ways we can we help each other "to grasp how wide and long and high and deep is the love of Christ"

5. List below some Christians you know and pray for them the way Paul does for the Ephesians.

**5**

Unity, diversity & Maturity

If you've ever watched a symphony orchestra playing you would appreciate that diversity is a beautiful thing. In an orchestra there is considerable diversity–different people playing different notes on different instruments made out of different materials. But when it all comes together there is a wonderful harmony, a much richer harmony than if they had all been playing exactly the same notes on exactly the same instruments.

The harmony that can be achieved through the diversity of an orchestra is a good illustration of what the apostle Paul now starts to consider in his letter to the Ephesian church. Paul has told us that when we are in Christ we are part of a wonderful new community of God (2:11-21). Having described God's new society, the apostle now describes the new standards expected in God's society. In particular, Paul gets the ball rolling by explaining how our corporate identity in Christ should influence how we treat each other.

It's important to also note that Paul is now entering a new phase in his letter. Up until now, Paul has been preoccupied with what God has done for us, but now he starts to tell us what we should be doing for God. That's what Christianity is all about. First come God's actions and then comes our response. Being a Christian is not about doing things to initiate God's favour. Being a Christian is responding to what God has already graciously done for us in Christ.

Investigate

Read Ephesians 4:1-6

1. What is the calling we have received (v.1)?

2. What do you consider to be Paul's main point in these verses? Is there a single verse which is a good summary of the section?

3. What does Paul mean by "one baptism"? (v.5)

4. When is it hard to be humble and gentle? (v.2)

5. What might be involved in "bearing with one another in love"? (v.2)

Our unity

Ephesians 4 opens with Paul focusing on the unity that we share in Christ. Paul states the obvious fact that Christians should have a unity because we have all been called by the same God. Just as we have a sense of affinity with those people in the same sporting team as us or in the same department at work as us, Christians should also have a sense of belonging to each other because we follow the same God. It doesn't matter whether a Christian goes to a Presbyterian or an Anglican or a Baptist or whatever brand of fellowship; Christians share a genuine unity because of the very nature of God and what he has done for us.

Note, however, that Paul says we will need to work hard at our unity with each other. Expressing our unity will require "every effort" (v.3). Christian fellowship is not immune from tensions. Indeed, it's exactly when fellowship starts to get personal and we start to open up our lives to each other that we become vulnerable to hurts, irritations and divisions.

Our unity in Christ should smother any differences we share like a blanket smothers a fire. We are God's new society. We are a humanity characterized not by a wall of hostility and division but by unity and peace (see study 3).

Paul doesn't end here. Yes, we have unity but we're not all clones. Yes, there is only one faith but our unity doesn't equal uniformity. There are differences between Christians and this too is part of God's kindness to us.

Investigate

Read Ephesians 4:7-13

1. What do these verses say about our differences as Christians?

2. Paul mentions several specific gifts in verse 11. Why do you think he does that?

3. What's the difference between spiritual blessings and spiritual gifts?

4. Who are to do "works of service" (v.12)? Is this the way we usually think about church?

5. What does Paul believe that the body of Christ will become? (vv.12-13)

Our diversity

Look around your church and you'll find that there are no two Christians the same. We are all different and Paul says that's exciting! Since we are all different, we all need each other.

Just as an orchestra only reaches a rich harmony through a range of different instruments, a Christian group can only find a rich unity through all its members contributing in their own different ways. Some of us are good musicians; some have an eye for detail and are good at administration and coordinating activities; others have personal skills that relax people and put them at ease; some people are good at explaining and teaching things. Christians are different and when we are put together we produce a harmony and a unity which just couldn't be achieved otherwise.

That's why Paul stresses that we are all to be doing works of service (v.12). We shouldn't go to a church like a sponge, waiting for what we can soak up. We meet with other Christians to do works of service so as to enhance our corporate unity and to encourage each other in our Christian maturity.

Investigate

Read Ephesians 4:14-16

1. What different illustrations does Paul use to depict a mature church? How are these illustrations helpful?

2. What roles do truth and love have in building maturity? What happens if either one of these is lacking?

3. What do you think it means to "grow up into him, who is the Head, that is Christ"? (v.15)

Our maturity

Paul closes this section by giving us an exciting picture of what a mature church looks like. It is a fellowship of people who speak the truth in love. People use their gifts to serve each other rather than to win praise and gratify themselves. People have a unity grounded in truth and not sentimentality. People are stable and firm, not rushing from one Christian fashion to the next.

A church like that would be a joy to be part of. A church like that will only ever happen if we build others up in love (v.16).

Think it through

1. Paul has encouraged us to make "every effort to keep the unity of the Spirit". What might some of these efforts be?

2. Why is it that our differences tend to divide churches rather than enhance them?

3. Paul has said a lot about unity in these verses. What role, if any, do you think exists for denominations?

4. "The trouble with the modern tendency for churches to work together is that it so often undermines important gospel truths." Do you agree? When can a desire for unity become unhelpful?

5. What contemporary warnings are there for us in v.14?

6. If we are all to do works of service (v.12) what role, if any, is there for ordained ministers?

7. What are some practial ways we can do 'works of service' for the people of our church:

    • on Sundays?

    • the rest of the week?

8. Are there any needs in your church that you think you could help fill? How might you go about that?

6

Ephesians 4:17 – 5:21

Walk this way

One of the exciting things about Ephesians is the way it describes the grandeur of what happens when we follow Jesus Christ. In Christ we become a new person. We have gone from spiritual rags to spiritual riches. We become members of God's new society. The Holy Spirit himself lives within us.

In our last study, we also discovered the exciting new lifestyle that should accompany our new identity in Christ. In particular Paul focused on the issues of our unity and diversity.

In this study we will consider Ephesians 4:17-5:21. Paul continues to expand on what type of lifestyle is worthy of the calling we have received. Now the focus falls onto personal godliness.

This is a long section with lots of ideas and it is easy to get lost in all the different things said. One helpful way of studying these verses is to focus on four illustrations which Paul uses to describe a Christian. Paul uses four everyday experiences:

- getting dressed;
- being part of a family;
- night and day; and
- someone drinking too much wine.

Paul uses each of these to illustrate what our new life in Christ should be like.

The key word in all this is the word "walk" (4:17, 5:2, 5:8, 5:15). You will see this word if you are using one of the more literal Bible versions (like the NASB). Other versions (like the NIV) often translate it as "live". It is a word which captures the everyday progress of our lives; the way we go about things as we travel on life's journey. The same word is used back in 2:2 and 2:10 in describing the contrast between our former existence ('walking' according to the ways of this world) and the new lifestyle that is ours in Christ (the good works which God has prepared for us to 'walk' in). It is also found in the opening verse of chapter 4, with its broad exhortation for us to 'walk' in a manner worthy of our calling.

In this passage, each time Paul uses that distinctive word 'walk', it introduces a slightly new section which revolves around a fresh illustration. Let's discover how it works.

Walk...
...not as the Gentiles do (4:17)

In this section Paul says that changing our lifestyle is like changing our clothes. You take off some things and you put other things on. Consider for example, a prisoner who has finally been released from jail after serving his time. The prisoner will discard his prison clothes and put on ordinary street clothes to suit the new status of freedom.

We were prisoners of sin. We used to walk in the ways of the world. We were dead and enslaved but God freed us (2:1-7). We should therefore put on a new lifestyle and new standards of behaviour which are appropriate to our new status. Its important to see that putting on the new lifestyle does not make us one of God's people. Simply taking off a prison uniform will not make a prisoner free from jail. God first frees us, through Jesus, and then in response the appropriate thing to do is to walk differently–to live a new lifestyle.

Investigate

Read Ephesians 4:17-31
1. How did we come to know Christ? What implication does this have on the way we should live?

2. List all the things which Paul says we should discard.

3. What things should we put on?

4. Why do we find it so hard to say only what is helpful for building others up (v.29)?

5. What are some practical ways that we can follow Paul's advice in verses 26-7?

Walk...
...in love (5:2)

In 5:2, Paul leaves the image of putting things off and on, and moves on to the image of having a family likeness. In Christ we are one of God's children, and so we should share the family likeness. We should live the sort of life which will provoke others to say: "Wow those people must be related to God. You can just see it in the way they live. They are so much like Jesus."

In particular, Paul focuses on two characteristics of Jesus—that he lived a life of love and that his life was a fragrant offering to God. If we have the divine family likeness we also should reflect these characteristics.

Investigate

Read Ephesians 4:32-5:7

1. What does it mean to "walk in love" or "live a life of love"? How did Jesus exemplify it?

2. In verses 3-7, Paul seems to be giving examples of what can stop us being a fragrant offering to God. What things does Paul mention?

3. In what sense is an immoral, impure or greedy person an idolater? (v.5)

Walk...
...as children of the light (5:8).

The third image Paul uses to describe our new life in Christ is the image of light and darkness. Walking in the dark is quite a different experience to walking in the hard, clear light of day. At night we walk cautiously, furtively, even secretly. A lifestyle of darkness is one which is shameful and needs to be hidden, but a lifestyle of light abounds in goodness and righteousness. It has nothing to hide and is happy to be seen by all.

In other words there ought to be no actions, motives or secret fantasies that we'd prefer others not to know about. It's actually not a bad way of testing our actions. Would you rent that video if you knew the whole Bible study group was going to watch it with you? Would you say those things about someone if you knew that person would hear them?

Those in Christ live a life so full of righteousness that they would be happy to be seen in the light.

Investigate

Read Ephesians 5:8-14

1. What are some fruitless deeds of darkness (v.11)? What do you think Paul means by telling us to "expose" them?

2. How can we find out what pleases the Lord? (v.10)

Walk...
...not as unwise but as wise (5:15).

In his fourth and final image, Paul outlines the new influences that should direct our new life. The image he uses is the way alcohol affects. Just as too much wine can affect our thinking and cause us to do things we might not normally do, Christians should let the Holy Spirit affect our thinking and cause us to do things we might not normally do. Someone who is drunk 'walks' like a fool– stumbling, staggering, and unable to speak properly. This is not how we should walk, says Paul.

Investigate

Read Ephesians 5:15-21

1. Verses 19-21 are actually all one sentence which outline four characteristics of being filled with the Spirit. What are these characteristics? What do they each mean?

   •

   •

   •

   •

2. What do you think Paul means in verse 16?

Be what you are!

We've looked at a big section of Ephesians in this study. It is easy to get lost in all the specifics and details but the big thought is very straightforward. Does our lifestyle reflect that we are new people in Christ?

We are to walk in a manner worthy of our calling. We are to live positively, knowing that, through his Spirit, God continues his good work in us. We are to live with a real excitement knowing that holiness is what we were chosen for all along (1:4). We are to put on our new clothes, show the family likeness, live in the light and be filled with the Spirit. We are to be who we are in Christ.

Think it through

1. Can you think of some other things not mentioned by Paul which should characterise our new lifestyle in Christ?

2. Is there any one verse which stands out from this section for you? Why?

3. What changes do you need to make as a result of reading this part of Scripure?

4. How does Paul's description of being filled with the Spirit compare with many contemporary ideas?

5. If we're saved by grace anyway, why do any of the things Paul says here really matter?

7 — Ephesians 5:21 – 6:9

After You!

If you were to rate parts of the Bible according to their popularity, the part of Ephesians which we are about to study would probably be close to the bottom of the list. These are verses which talk about wives submitting to their husbands as the head of the family, children obeying their parents and slaves fearing their masters. In a world where children can now divorce their parents and popular culture demands equality between men and women, this section of the Bible is often seen as old fashioned, out of date and irrelevant to modern society. I personally know of a minister who, when preaching through this section in church, refused to read out Ephesians 5:21-24 on the basis that society had moved on from such archaic views.

It's a tragedy when people overlook this wonderful part of the Bible, because tucked away in these verses are some of the most exhilarating and fulfilling truths of the Bible.

The principle of submission

The section we are looking at in this study is 5:21-6:9. These verses talk about husband-wife relationships, parent-child relationships and slave-master relationships. At first glance it would seem to be a fairly diverse passage but the overarching principle is found in 5:21, "Submit to one another out of reverence for Christ".

In our last study, we discovered that this principle of submission was one of the characteristics of being filled with the Spirit. Having stated that truth in 5:21, Paul now launches into a long section in which he describes how submitting to others will work out in different situations. In other words, this whole section is about how submission transforms the roles we have and the tasks we do in life.

When we understand Paul's logic in this way it actually raises the stakes about what is said in these verses. Submission in our different relationships is not an archaic attitude which is now out of fashion. It is actually one of the ways we identify ourselves as being a Spirit-filled person.

Investigate

Read Ephesians 5:22-33

1. How should wives relate to their husbands?

Submit in everything

2. How should husbands treat their wives? What goals should a husband have?

make her Holy
give himself up for
love as own bodies/feed/care

3. How should Christians relate to Christ? How does this help wives understand their role?

Headship model
does this help?

4. How does Christ relate to his Church? How does this help husbands understand their role?

Make her Holy
cleansing

The practice of submission

Before we can properly see the beauty of this section of Ephesians we need to clear away some dead wood. We need to expose some common ideas which are godless and which only serve to confuse the issue.

TRUTH #1: different roles do not mean different values

Many people think that having a different role means that you also have a different importance. We are all ranked in the social pecking order in which a doctor is more important than a street sweeper and a solicitor is more important than a milk man. This way of thinking is *completely foreign to God.* Back in Ephesians 1-2 Paul has explained the way God thinks. We are all failures and rebels who have been forgiven in Christ. We might be a prime minister or a plumber or a housewife or a university graduate or an unskilled labourer, and it makes no difference to our value to God. We may not be identical but we are equal in value.

TRUTH #2: submission does not mean inferiority

Most of us are so preoccupied with standing up for personal rights these days that we feel if we ever forego our rights to someone, the other person is therefore more important than us. Why else would you submit to someone else unless you had to because he or she was more important than you? The reverse is also true—if ever we are in authority over someone else, we tend to think that it says something about how very important and superior we are.

Again God thinks in a radically different way. Greatness in the Kingdom of God is measured by servanthood. Jesus himself came not to be served but to serve. Jesus submitted to his Father's will, and died our death on the cross, even though he is the one to whom all creation will bend the knee (see study 1). His greatness and authority was seen in the way he laid down his life for his people.

This relates to marriage. It is God's design that marriage works best when a husband and wife have different roles. God has intended that the husband be the leader and head of the house, and that the wife gladly submit to his leadership (vv.22-23). Left to our own sinful nature these roles can quickly degenerate into chauvinism, feminism, selfishness and arguing. But when a couple is living under the influence of the Spirit and mutually serving one another, these roles complement each other. The husband takes the lead, but not in an overbearing or selfish way. Like Christ dying for his church, his sole concern is to love his wife, and lay down his life for her. The wife follows this lead and supports her husband in it. She gladly submits, as she does to Christ—not in menial servitude and oppressed silence, but in love and respect and unity. The marriage grows to joyous levels of intimacy and strength.

Investigate

Read Ephesians 6:1-4

1. What different roles does God intend for parents and children?

C — obey Honour

P — dont exasperate / Train + Instruct

2. What reasons are given for children obeying parents?

10 Com + promise

3. Paul specifically mentions fathers in verse 4. Do you think that it's equally valid to apply the verse to mothers?

If he is head — Exasperation will often come from him.

Read Ephesians 6:5-9

4. What different responsibilities exist for

• slaves?

[handwritten: obey respect Fear Sincerity win favour with them + God]

• masters?

[handwritten: Some – Don't Threaten]

5. How should their relationship with Christ affect their behaviour towards one another:

• slaves?

• masters?

The pleasure of submission

It's a shame that submission is so misunderstood and unpopular, because the biblical pattern of relationships is a source of incredible pleasure, fulfilment and contentment. When we start to live out our life's role in godly submission and love, we experience more joy than we can imagine.

A family in which parents and children are committed to one another, such that the children obey their parents, and the parents care for the children in tenderness without exasperating them—this is the sort of family that anyone would envy. A marriage in which a husband expresses his leadership in the home by laying down his life for his wife, and in which a wife gladly and lovingly submits to this leadership–this is a relationship more intimate and secure than romantic Hollywood movies can begin to imagine. Even a master-slave relationship would be a joy to be in when both master and slave work out their respective roles with the welfare of the other in mind.

Submission is not old fashioned. It is a desperately needed ingredient in our modern world. Submission is not a sign of inferiority or weakness. It's a sign of being filled with the Spirit.

Think it through

1. Why is it so hard to put other people before ourselves?

We might miss out on stuff.
No-one might put us first

2. What are some specific ways in which a husband can love his wife and lay down his life for her?

3. What current attitudes tend to work against a wife submitting to her husband?

"equality"

4. Is it ever right to disobey your parents?

Y

5. Give some examples of the ways parents can exasperate their children?

Not take into consid.
their stage.

6. What relevance does the teaching about masters and slaves have to our modern work environment?

work for the Lord.

8

Living in the War Zone

There is a major conspiracy going on. Increasing numbers of people are believing a dangerous lie. The lie is that the occult is harmless.

For many people the devil is a bit of a joke; just an imaginary guy in a red suit holding a pitch fork. A few years ago, a magazine ran an article entitled *Consumer's Guide to Hell.* It surveyed people's beliefs about the supernatural, and of all those questioned, only one third of those who believed in heaven also believed in the devil. Satan has clearly fooled a lot of people.

At the end of Paul's letter to the Ephesians, the apostle wants to make sure that his readers are under no illusions about the reality and seriousness of the forces of evil. Paul wants his readers to understand that being a Christian is not a life of leisure. It is not even just hard work. To be a Christian is to be at war. What's worse, it is a dirty war where there are no rules. It is a subversive war where apparently little things can ultimately bring us down.

Investigate

Read Ephesians 6:10-13

1. Why do you think Paul closes his letter with this warning?

2. Why do you think the powers of darkness want to wage war on us? (Eph 3:10; Col 2:13-15)

3. What are some of the "devil's schemes"?

4. What do we have to do to protect ourselves from the evil forces?

Taking Satan too seriously

At one extreme, some people don't take Satan seriously enough; at the other, many Christians take him far too seriously. Many churches become too preoccupied with Satan and mistakenly believe that he has more power than he does.

For the Christian, Satan has been stripped of his power. All we have to do against the devil is to stand! Don't go looking for him. Don't go asking for a fight. Don't seek out exorcism opportunities. Simply be strong in the Lord, have confidence in what God has done for us and stand firm. As James says, resist the devil and he will flee (Jas 4:7). In other words, forget the movies about objects being thrown about the room and heads spinning round. The only power the devil has is the power we give him when we believe his lies. Just resist him. Be strong and you will triumph. That's because God's children are protected by the armour of God.

So what exactly is this armour?

Investigate

Read Ephesians 6:13-17

1. List below all the different pieces of the armour of God. What does each represent?

2. *Look up Ephesians 1:13.* What pieces of the armour are mentioned in this verse? (Many Bibles use the word "believed" in 1:13, but it is exactly the same word that is translated "faith" in 6:16.) What does this verse tell us about the armour of God?

The armour of God

The first thing to notice about the armour of God is that it is the armour of God. God provides it! All we have to do is slip it on and stand firm. The armour, therefore, is not so much something we have to do as something that God has done. We simply have to avail ourselves of it.

Understood in that sense, the armour of God is a picture of the gospel. All the pieces of armour mentioned are references to different aspects of the gospel. Truth, righteousness, the gospel of peace, faith, salvation, Spirit; they are all different perspectives of the good news that Christ died for our sins on the cross.

So when Paul says to put on the full armour of God, he is telling us to stand firm in the gospel. Don't desert the gospel. Don't wander from Jesus. Surround yourself in what Jesus Christ has done for you.

In other words, it is the gospel that defeats the devil.

The Bible refers to Satan as a liar, a tempter and an accuser. He tempts people into sin by lying to them, and when we fall for his lies he stands before God and accuses us. The gospel robs him of this power. Satan can accuse us before God until he is blue in the face, but when we are in Christ we are forgiven and reconciled with God.

That's why the devil hates the gospel. It cuts his legs from under him, and he will do anything to lure us away from it. Paul is only too aware of this. He warns his readers to stand firm in the gospel. He also tells them to pray.

Investigate

Read Ephesians 6:18-24

1. What does it mean to pray "in the Spirit"? How does verse 17 help us understand this phrase? (Think also about what it means to be filled with the Spirit in 5:18.)

2. Why does Paul encourage his readers to be alert in verse 18? About what does he want them to be alert?

3. About what does Paul ask for prayer?

4. What is the mystery of the gospel in verse 19? (See study 3 for a reminder.)

The power of prayer

The very fact that one of Paul's final requests in the letter is for prayer should alert us to the importance of prayer. When you are in a spiritual battle, it's crazy not to keep in close contact with your spiritual commander in chief!

We need to pray. We need to pray for our non-Christian friends and family who are still dead in their sins and far from God. We need to pray for those who are tricked by the devil's schemes into thinking that the gospel is nonsense. We need to pray that God will release them by revealing the mystery of the gospel.

We need to pray for each other. We need to pray that we might not fall for the devil's scheme ourselves and that nothing would come between us and the gospel. We need to pray that we will stand firm.

Stand firm

It is a dirty war that the devil wages. We mustn't fall into the trap of thinking that being a Christian is a game. The forces of evil are marshalled against us to try and make us desert the gospel. Lies will come into our heads, suggesting that Jesus is not worth the effort. Doubt and temptation will make us think that reading the Bible and spending time in prayer aren't all that important. We will be tempted to complete this study book, learn a few things, but never actually change our lives.

At the end of this mighty letter, God is calling us to arms. We are in a war. He is saying to us: Recognise the subversive acts of the enemy. Identify the temptations that might lead you away from the gospel. Be aware of seemingly innocent things which can start to weaken your faith. Take your stand against everything that might seduce you away from Christianity.

If you don't remember anything else from this study series on Ephesians, remember that through the gospel of our Lord Jesus Christ you have every spiritual blessing. Therefore put on the gospel and keep it on. Stand firm!

Think it through

1. What are some of the reasons that people desert the gospel?

2. What is the thing in your life that you think poises the greatest threat to your faith? What steps can you take now to ensure that you will never desert the gospel?

3. How can we help each other to be "strong in the Lord"? (v.10)

4. What should we be praying for:

   • ourselves?

   • gospel preachers?

5. Ephesians is a very intense letter with many diverse ideas. Among all the things we've discovered throughout these studies, which truth has stuck most in your mind? Why?

Tips for Leaders

Studying Ephesians

The studies in *Walk this way* like all of the Interactive and Topical Bible Studies from Matthias Media, are aimed to fall somewhere between a sermon and a set of unadorned discussion questions. The idea is to provide a little more direction and information than you would normally see in a set of printed Bible studies, but to maintain an emphasis on personal investigation, thought, discovery and application. We aim to give input and help, without doing all the work for the reader/studier.

In many respects, Ephesians is a fairly straightforward epistle for group study, with many stirring passages of theology and practical application. The two studies most likely to prove difficult in group discussion are studies 1 and 7, for different reasons.

In Study 1, we dive straight into the deep and mysterious waters of predestination and election. The study does not attempt to focus particularly on these spiritual blessings, because neither does Paul—they are numbered among the many wonderful things that God has done for us in Christ. Be prepared for some lively discussion all the same:

• Don't be tempted to deny or sidestep what the Scripture is saying at this point. We should rejoice, as the apostle does.
• Be prepared to point to other parts of Scripture which affirm man's role and responsibility in salvation (such as all the things we are exhorted to do in chapters 4-6), while not pulling back from seeing God at work in all of it. Note how chapter 2:8-10 contains this balance—we respond in faith and live a life of good works, but even our response and lifestyle are due to God's gracious, creative power (cf. Phil 2:12-13).
• Don't attempt to say more than can be said, or apply this truth other than the apostle does (in order to draw comfort and joy). It is quite right to have an appropriate degree of humble silence before some of these mysteries.

In Study 7, we meet the controversial topic of men, women and submission. In many respects, the passage itself is quite straightforward and clear. The difficulties arise from how violently its teaching clashes with the prevailing views of Western culture. We have tried to address this conflict to some extent, without getting bogged down too much in what has sometimes been a heated and messy debate. As a group leader, you will need to do the same. To this end, it is important that you do at least two things:

• Carefully work through the issues in your own mind, and be prepared to stand for the truth; this may be difficult, but it is the only loving course.
• Be sensitive in the way you handle the discussion, realising that strong emotions are involved for many people.

Like all our studies, these are designed to work in a group on the assumption that the group members have worked through the material in advance. If this is not happening in your group it will obviously change the way you lead the session.

If the group is preparing...

If all is well, and the group is well-prepared, then reading through all the text, and answering all the questions will be time consuming and probably quite boring. It is not designed to work this way in a group.

The leader needs to go through the study thoroughly in advance and work out how to lead a group discussion using the text and questions as a basis. You should be able to follow the order of the study through pretty much as it is written. But you will need to work out which things you are going to omit, which you are going to glide over quite quickly, and which you are going to concentrate on and perhaps add supplementary discussion questions to.

Obviously, as with all studies, this process of selection and augmentation will be based on what your aims are for this study for your particular group. You need to work out where you want to get to as a main emphasis or teaching point or application point at the end. The material itself will certainly head you in a certain direction, but there will usually be various emphases you can bring out, and a variety of applications to think about.

The slabs of text need to be treated as a resource for discussion, not something to be simply read out. This will mean highlighting portions to talk about, adding supplementary discussion questions and ideas to provoke discussion where you think that would be helpful for your particular group, and so on.

The same is true for the 'investigate' and 'think it through' questions. You need to be selective, according to where you want the whole thing to go. Some questions you will want to do fairly quickly or omit altogether. Others you will want to concentrate on—because they are difficult or because they are crucial or both—and in these cases you may want to add a few questions of your own if you

think it would help.

You may also need to add some probing questions of your own if your group is giving too many 'pat' answers, or just reproducing the ideas in the text sections without actually grappling with the biblical text for themselves.

There is room for flexibility. Some groups, for example, read the text and do the 'investigate' questions in advance, but save the 'think it through' questions for the group discussion.

If the group isn't preparing...

This obviously makes the whole thing a lot harder (as with any study). Most of the above still applies. But if your group is not doing much preparation, your role is even more crucial and active. You will have to be even more careful in your selection and emphasis and supplementary questions—you will have to convey the basic content, as well as develop it in the direction of personal application. Reading through the whole study in the group will still be hard going. In your selection, you will probably need to read more sections of text together (selecting the important bits), and will not be able to glide over comprehension questions so easily.

If the group is not preparing, it does make it harder—not impossible, but a good reason for encouraging your group to do at least some preparation.

Conclusion

No set of printed studies can guarantee a good group learning experience. No book can take the place of a well-prepared thoughtful leader who knows where he or she wants to take the group, and guides them gently along that path.

Our Bible studies aim to be a resource and handbook for that process. They will do a lot of the work for you. All the same, they need to be *used* not simply followed.

Interactive and Topical Bible Studies

Our Interactive Bible Studies (IBS) and Topical Bible Studies (TBS) are a valuable resource to help you keep feeding from God's Word. The IBS series works through passages and books of the Bible; the TBS series pulls together the Bible's teaching on topics, such as money or prayer. As at July 2001, the series contains the following titles:

OLD TESTAMENT

FULL OF PROMISE
(THE BIG PICTURE OF THE O.T.)
Authors: Phil Campbell
& Bryson Smith, 8 studies

BEYOND EDEN
(GENESIS 1-11)
Authors: Phillip Jensen
and Tony Payne, 9 studies

THE ONE AND ONLY
(DEUTERONOMY)
Author: Bryson Smith,
8 studies

THE GOOD, THE BAD & THE UGLY (JUDGES)
Author: Mark Baddeley
10 studies

FAMINE & FORTUNE
(RUTH)
Authors: Barry Webb &
David Hohne, 4 studies

THE EYE OF THE STORM
(JOB)
Author: Bryson Smith,
6 studies

TWO CITIES
(ISAIAH)
Authors: Andrew Reid and
Karen Morris, 9 studies

KINGDOM OF DREAMS
(DANIEL)
Authors: Andrew Reid and
Karen Morris, 8 studies

BURNING DESIRE
(OBADIAH & MALACHI)
Authors: Phillip Jensen and
Richard Pulley, 6 studies

NEW TESTAMENT

THE GOOD LIVING GUIDE
(MATTHEW 5:1-12)
Authors: Phillip Jensen
and Tony Payne, 9 studies

NEWS OF THE HOUR
(MARK)
Author: Peter Bolt,
10 studies

FREE FOR ALL
(GALATIANS)
Authors: Phillip Jensen
& Kel Richards, 8 studies

WALK THIS WAY
(EPHESIANS)
Author: Bryson Smith,
8 studies

THE COMPLETE CHRISTIAN
(COLOSSIANS)
Authors: Phillip Jensen
and Tony Payne, 8 studies

ALL LIFE IS HERE
(1 TIMOTHY)
Authors: Phillip Jensen
and Greg Clarke, 9 studies

RUN THE RACE
(2 TIMOTHY)
Author: Bryson Smith,
6 studies

THE PATH TO GODLINESS
(TITUS)
Authors: Phillip Jensen
and Tony Payne, 6 studies

THE IMPLANTED WORD
(JAMES)
Authors: Phillip Jensen
and K.R. Birkett, 8 studies

HOMEWARD BOUND
(1 PETER)
Authors: Phillip Jensen and
Tony Payne, 10 studies

ALL YOU NEED TO KNOW
(2 PETER)
Author: Bryson Smith,
6 studies

TOPICAL BIBLE STUDIES

BOLD I APPROACH
(PRAYER)
Author: Tony Payne,
6 studies

CASH VALUES
(MONEY)
Author: Tony Payne,
5 studies

THE BLUEPRINT
(DOCTRINE)
Authors: Phillip Jensen
& Tony Payne, 11 studies

WOMAN OF GOD
Author: Terry Blowes
8 studies

THE MAN WHO MAKES A DIFFERENCE (EPHESIANS)
Author: Tony Payne
7 studies
This set of studies from Ephesians, is designed especially for men, and is sold as a separate leaders' guide and study guide